Derek Jeter

By Sandy Donovan

AMAZING
ATHLETES

LERNER**SPORTS** / **Minneapolis**

This book is available in two editions:
Library binding by LernerSports
Soft cover by First Avenue Editions
Imprints of Lerner Publishing Group
241 First Avenue North
Minneapolis, MN 55401 U.S.A.

Website address: www.lernerbooks.com

Library of Congress Cataloging-in-Publication Data

Donovan, Sandy, 1967–
    Derek Jeter / by Sandy Donovan.
      p.   cm.—(Amazing athletes)
    Summary: Introduces the life and accomplishments of champion baseball player Derek Jeter, shortstop for the New York Yankees. Includes bibliographical references and index.
    ISBN: 0–8225–3674–9 (lib. bdg. : alk. paper)
    ISBN: 0–8225–2038–9 (pbk. : alk. paper)
    1. Jeter, Derek, 1974– —Juvenile literature. 2. Baseball players—United States—Biography—Juvenile literature. [1. Jeter, Derek, 1974– 2. Baseball players. 3. Racially mixed people—Biography.] I. Title. II. Series.
    GV865.J48D66 2004
    796.357'092—dc22
                                      2003015413

Manufactured in the United States of America
1 2 3 4 5 6 – DP – 09 08 07 06 05 04

TABLE OF CONTENTS

During the 2000 World Series, fans rode the subway between New York City's two baseball hubs, Yankee Stadium in the Bronx and Shea Stadium in Queens. It was the city's first "subway series" since 1956.

WORLD SERIES HERO

In October 2000, New York City was buzzing. The two hometown baseball teams, the Yankees and the Mets, were facing each other in the **World Series.** The Yankees were led by their superstar shortstop, Derek Jeter.

Derek and the Yankees were trying to win their third straight World Series. The team was on a roll. Derek was the biggest superstar on a team loaded with star players. He always seemed to come through when the game was on the line.

Derek *(second from right)* takes to the field with some teammates to warm up for Game One of the 2000 World Series.

Derek gets a bear hug from teammate Jose Vizcaino, as the Yankees celebrate winning Game One.

This series was no different. Derek opened Game Four by knocking the first pitch he saw over the fence for a **home run.** The Yankees won the game 3–2. Late in Game Five, Derek hit another home run to tie the game. The Yankees went on to win that game too.

Since the first World Series in 1903, the New York Yankees have won the championship twenty-six times.

The Yankees won the Series four games to one. Derek was named the World Series Most Valuable Player. In the series, Derek had nine hits in 22 **at-bats,** for a .409 **batting average.** He hit two **doubles,** a **triple,** and two home runs. Derek had been with the Yankees for five years. In those years, the team had won the World Series four times.

Sports Illustrated magazine gave Derek an Outstanding Achievement Award for his performance in the 2000 World Series.

Derek began his baseball career in the Little Leagues.

Young Yankees Fan

Derek Jeter was always a New York Yankees fan. He was born on June 26, 1974, in Pequannock, New Jersey, not far from New York City. His whole family—parents, grandparents, aunts, uncles, and cousins—were Yankees fans.

When Derek was four years old, he moved to Kalamazoo, Michigan, with his mother, Dorothy, and father, Charles. But Derek's love for the Yankees stayed with him. He covered his new bedroom with Yankees posters. He wore his blue Yankees jacket every day.

Some of baseball's greatest players have worn the Yankees' pinstriped uniform. They include Babe Ruth, Joe DiMaggio, Lou Gehrig, Mickey Mantle, Reggie Jackson, and Roger Clemens. Yankee great Dave Winfield was one of Derek's favorite players.

Every summer, Derek visited his grandparents in New Jersey. When he was six, his grandmother took him to his first game at Yankee Stadium.

But Derek wanted to be more than a Yankees fan. He wanted to be a Yankees player. In his eighth-grade yearbook, he wrote that he would play for the Yankees one day. Playing for the Yankees was Derek's **goal.**

Derek told his parents that he wanted to play shortstop for the Yankees. They told him he would have to work hard to reach this goal.

But they said he could not just focus on baseball. He had to work hard at school too.

Derek did work hard. In high school, he got mostly A's. He practiced baseball every day. His family helped him. Dorothy, Charles, and Derek's younger sister, Sharlee, would play ball with him for hours.

Derek's father, Charles, sister, Sharlee, and mother, Dorothy, are Derek's biggest fans.

Derek was considered one of the best high school baseball players in the country.

BECOMING A YANKEE

In high school, Derek was a star baseball player. During his last two seasons, he hit better than .500. **Scouts** for **major league** teams came to see him play in nearly every game. Some scouts thought Derek was the best high school player in the country.

Many high school coaches felt the same way. In his senior year, Derek was named the 1992 Player of the Year by the American Baseball Coaches Association. It looked like he would be **drafted** by, or picked to join, a major league organization.

Every year, Major League Baseball holds a draft. Each team takes turns drafting players. In 1992, the Cincinnati Reds had the first pick. Many people thought the Reds would choose Derek.

The Yankees drafted Derek soon after he graduated from high school.

But the Reds picked a different player. Instead, Derek got a surprise phone call. The New York Yankees called to say they had drafted him. Derek could not believe it. Was his dream of playing for the Yankees about to come true?

Minor league teams have different classes. Young, inexperienced players usually begin on a Class A team. As they get better, they move to Class AA. Class AAA teams are the closest step to the major leagues.

Hundreds of players are drafted each year. But only a few make it to the major leagues. Derek knew he would have to work hard in the **minor leagues** to earn a spot with the Yankees.

Derek went to play for the Yankees' Class A

team, the Tampa Yankees. He was full of excitement. But he was soon homesick for his family. He had never been so far away from them.

Derek had a rocky start in the minor leagues. During his first two years, he struggled with his batting and fielding. But Derek worked hard and became a better player. In 1994, the Yankees moved him up to their Class AA team. His batting average soared to .377. He was becoming a whiz at shortstop too. Derek was beginning to look like a star.

Over three million people a year attend home games at Yankee Stadium.

ROOKIE OF THE YEAR

By 1995, Derek was playing for the Yankees' Class AAA team. That season, he also got his first taste of the big leagues. Derek played fifteen games for the Yankees. After the season, he was determined to make it back to the big leagues. That winter break, he practiced every day. During **spring training,**

Derek impressed Yankees manager Joe Torre so much that Torre gave Derek the starting shortstop job.

Derek quickly proved that Torre had made the right choice. During the first game of the 1996 season, Derek smashed a home run over the left field fence. He also made a difficult over-the-shoulder catch. His plays helped the Yankees beat the Cleveland Indians.

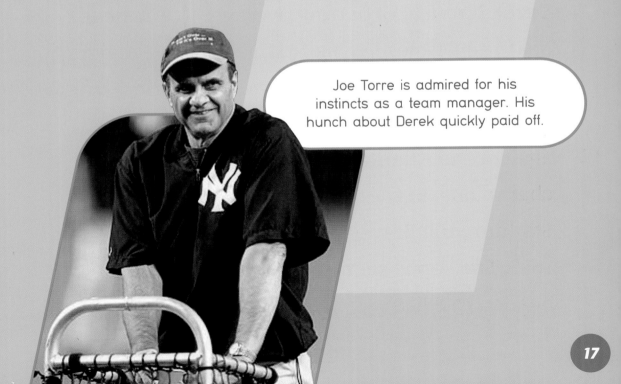

Joe Torre is admired for his instincts as a team manager. His hunch about Derek quickly paid off.

Derek continued to impress fans and players in his rookie year. In July, he got a hit in seventeen straight games. His skill at the plate and on the field helped carry the Yankees to the **play-offs**. In the American League Championship against the Baltimore Orioles, Derek had a .412 batting average. The Yankees beat the Orioles. In his first year in the majors, Derek helped lead his team to the World Series.

In 1996, Derek became the first rookie in thirty-four years to be the Yankees' starting shortstop.

The Yankees went to the 1996 World Series against the Atlanta Braves, the defending champions. In the first two games at Yankee Stadium, the Braves outscored the Yankees 16–1. The series seemed lost as the Yankees headed to Atlanta for the next three games.

But the Yankees bounced back and won all three games in Atlanta. Back in New York, the Yankees won Game Six. It was their first World Championship since 1978. Derek was voted Rookie of the Year.

Derek cheers as the Yankees tag out another Brave during the 1996 World Series.

Derek signs autographs for fans at
Fenway Park in Boston.

OFF THE FIELD

Derek became one of the most popular
Yankees. Letters from baseball fans piled up in
his locker. But Derek wanted to make a
difference off the field as well as on it.

After the 1996 season, Derek began a new
project. He started the Turn 2 Foundation. (To
"turn 2" means to make a **double play** in

baseball.) Derek's group raises money to help keep kids away from drugs. It encourages kids to be healthy and to do well in school. The foundation has started after-school programs, park festivals, and scholarships.

Derek wanted to show kids with problems at home or in school that they could work for success. Derek's father, Charles, is Turn 2's director. Derek said he has always looked up to his father. Charles worked for years helping other people as a drug and alcohol counselor.

Charles and Derek work together on the Turn 2 Foundation's programs.

Derek jokes with friend and fellow shortstop Alex Rodriguez.

Derek's work in the community is an important part of his life. "People look up to you if you play for the Yankees," he said. "I think you should do something to help out. Off the field is when people look up to you even more."

In 1997, Derek and the rest of the Yankees had a good year. They made the play-offs but lost to the Cleveland Indians in the first round. Still, Derek was proud of his team, and he was proud of his community work. He kept practicing to improve his play on the field. When they arrived for spring training in 1998, Derek and the Yankees were ready for a big year.

Derek fields a ground ball during spring training. The Yankees train in Tampa, Florida, at Legends Field.

Derek and Cleveland Indians shortstop Omar Vizquel goof off before the 1999 All-Star Game.

SHORTSTOP SUPERSTAR

Derek and the Yankees steamrolled through the league in 1998, winning 114 games. Derek hit 19 home runs. He also led the American League in runs scored, with 127.

The Yankees went on to the 1998 World Series. They swept the San Diego Padres to win the championship.

In 1999, Derek's batting average zoomed to .349. He led the American League in hits, at 219. Once again, the Yankees rolled to the World Series. They again faced the Atlanta Braves. They swept the Braves in four tough games. It was the twenty-fifth World Championship for the New York Yankees. The city held a huge celebration for its baseball heroes.

Derek fires a shot to first base during the 1999 World Series.

Derek celebrates the 1999 World Series victory with Yankees fans, spraying the crowd with champagne.

In 2000, Derek and the Yankees beat the New York Mets for their third straight World Championship. They became the first major league team in almost thirty years to "three-peat." Derek had a hit in fourteen straight World Series games, one of the longest hitting streaks ever.

In 2001, Derek got on base in twenty-five of the first twenty-six games. The Yankees again made it to the World Series. They were expected to win. But they lost to the Arizona Diamondbacks in a seven-game series.

During the 2002 season, Derek's batting average slipped to .297. But he hit 18 home runs and scored 124 runs.

Derek and the Yankees were disappointed when they lost the American League Division Series. But they were ready to work hard in 2003.

On opening day 2003, Derek injured his right shoulder. He missed thirty-six games. But in June, Yankees owner George Steinbrenner announced that Derek would be honored with a special title. He was named team captain.

Derek became the team's eleventh captain, following other Yankee greats such as Babe Ruth and Lou Gehrig.

Derek rebounded from his injury to hit .324, with 10 home runs and 52 runs batted in. He helped the Yankees clinch the American League Championship in a tough seven-game battle against the Boston Red Sox. The Yankees then squared off against the Florida Marlins in the World Series. In Game 3 Derek had three hits, including two doubles. But the Marlins won the World Championship in six games.

"They beat us," Derek said of the Marlins after the World Series. "No one deserves it more than they do."

It was a difficult loss for the Yankees. But Derek will be there as team captain as the Yankees plan for 2004. The Yankees recognize Derek's ability to lead and motivate his teammates, as well as his ability to play a great game of baseball.

Selected Career Highlights

2003 Named team captain

2002 Played on his fifth consecutive All-Star team
Collected his 1,200th career hit and 100th home run on opening
  day, April 1

2001 Scored his 500th run on April 23, becoming the fourth Yankee
  ever to reach 500 runs before his twenty-sixth birthday
Became the third Yankee ever to have more than 200 hits
  three years in a row

2000 Named All-Star Game MVP
Yankees beat their hometown rivals, the New York Mets, to win the
  World Series for the third year in a row.
Named World Series MVP

1999 Had a .349 batting average, second highest in the American
  League
Yankees swept the Atlanta Braves to win their twenty-fifth
  World Series.

1998 Hit 19 home runs, setting the record for single-season home
  runs by a Yankees' shortstop
Led the American League in runs scored with 127
Yankees set an American League record with 114
  wins in a single season.
Yankees swept the San Diego Padres in the World
  Series.

1997 Tied the American League high of 142 singles in
  a season

1996 Hit a home run on opening day
Won American League Rookie of the Year award

Glossary

at-bat: a batter's official turn at the plate during a game. If the batter walks, sacrifices, or is hit by a pitch, the turn is not counted as an at-bat.

batting average: a number that describes how often a baseball player makes a base hit

double play: a play in which two base runners are thrown or tagged out

doubles: plays in which the batter hits the ball and safely reaches second base

drafted: to be picked by a ball club to play on a team

goal: an accomplishment that a person works to achieve

home run: a hit that allows the batter to circle all the bases in one play to score a run

major league: the top group of professional baseball teams. Major League Baseball has two leagues, the American League and the National League. The New York Yankees play in the American League.

minor leagues: leagues ranked below the major league, in which players improve their playing skills and prepare to move to the majors

play-offs: a series of games played after a regular season to determine which teams will play in a championship

scouts: people who search around the country for talented baseball players. Scouts recommend players they think teams should try to draft or sign.

spring training: a period in the spring (February to April) when teams practice for the upcoming season

triple: a play in which the batter hits the ball and safely reaches third base

World Series: baseball's championship. In Major League Baseball, the National and American Leagues both hold their own league championships at the end of the regular season. The winning teams from each league meet each other in the World Series.

Further Reading & Websites

Christopher, Matt. *On the Field with Derek Jeter.* New York: Little, Brown, and Co., 2000.

Kasoff, Jerry. *Baseball Just for Kids: Skills, Strategies and Stories to Make You a Better Ballplayer.* New York: Grand Slam Press, 1996.

Rambeck, Richard. *The History of the New York Yankees.* Mankato, MN: Creative Education, 1998.

Major League Baseball
<http://www.mlb.com>
Major League Baseball's official website has baseball news, games, and events. The Kids section has interviews with star players and "Tips from the Pros." You can also learn where to send letters to your favorite players.

New York Yankees' Home Page
<http://newyork.yankees.mlb.com>
The official website of the New York Yankees features the latest news, as well as the history of the team. The Players section includes Derek Jeter's biography, statistics, and career highlights.

Turn 2 Foundation
<http://www.turn2foundation.org>
The official homepage of Derek Jeter's foundation includes a list of events and programs. A special kids' section features games, a photo flipbook, and a screen saver.

Index

Photo Acknowledgments

Photographs are used with the permission of: © Reuters NewMedia Inc./ CORBIS, pp. 4, 5, 6, 7, 20, 23, 25, 26; Turn 2 Foundation, Inc., p. 8; Jim Merihew/ Kalamazoo Gazette, p. 11; Classmates.com Yearbook Archive, pp. 12, 13; © Joseph Sohm; Visions of America/CORBIS, p. 16; © AFP/CORBIS, pp. 17, 24; SportsChrome East/West, Rob Tringali, Jr., p. 19; © John-Marshall Mantel/ CORBIS, p. 21; © John Klein, p. 22; © Chris Trotman/NewSport/CORBIS, p. 29.

Cover: © Michael Kim/CORBIS.